Matthew Schlueb **Villa Vuoto**

An Architect's Manifesto
on the Origin of Creativity

Stella Cadente Publications
Copyright © 2008 - 2010

ISBN: 1 451555 88 1
EAN-13: 978 1 451555 88 2
First Edition
532
544

Text and illustrations by
Matthew Schlueb

Front cover: Oskar on Villa Vuoto hillside,
the day an eagle flew over.

Back cover: glass curtain with distortions of
blue mosaics releasing memories of a grotto.

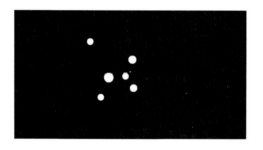

068

I was four.
At first, I was afraid and must have cried when my mom left me there. Though in retrospect, she probably never left. After some time past and I became conditioned to the space, the excitement of something new, different, unknown enticed me to play. A merry-go-round in a room of colors, I was stepping into a dreamy world, unlike any I had known before.

This is my earliest memory.

Much of my home was formed by my first day of pre-school. The circular space, the bold colors, the playful spirit materialized from memories in my head.

Villa Vuoto is the dream of a child.   Manifesto.

So I could live in my head.

422

When I take people through our home, I am often asked,
'Where did the design of this come from?'

The answer is not a simple one liner.
It requires some time to explain completely.

What is the source of an idea?

In the case of our home, there are several primary factors.
My childhood experiences,
things that inspire me,
the essential qualities of a home,
my creative design process,
and the origin of creativity itself.

This is my attempt to put into words these factors
and to elaborate on how they shaped Villa Vuoto.

Returning from pre-school, pulling up to the house, we startled a deer on the driveway. She leaped over the crest of the slope, out of sight.

"Be very quite" I told Oskar, "…and maybe we'll see her."
We inched toward the edge, looked over and sure enough, she was at the bottom of the hill, a statue looking right up at us. Oskar waved, I mimicked his lead, but she remained frozen. Not a twitch of her ear, not even the stabilizing of her wounded right rear leg, hoof just barely off the ground.

Suddenly I realized that her life was flashing before her eyes. We were terrifying. I was no longer in my son's head, sharing the wonders of the wilderness. I was in the deer's head, feeling her worries, panic, pleads. Instinctively, I raised my left hand, open palm and held it still, just long enough to catch her eye.

Then, I felt it. Unmistakable.

The tension in the air dissolved in an instant. The feeling spoke clearly. Confirmed by her gesture, solid as granite she melted, turned her head down and casually went on her way looking for more leaves to feed.

"Hold your hand up, like a native saying 'peace'."
Oskar did. "That way she will know you are a friend."
Hearing me speak, she looked back up again. Then continued, hopping away on three strong legs and one weak one.

We probably weren't the first people she has encountered.
But, this was our first encounter with her.

How did she understand my sign language?
What made me do it?
Had she seen that one before?

Maybe so. Most likely not.
But, her ancestral grandmothers might have.
Less than two centuries ago, the Shawano still walked these woods, trying not to alarm any doe, as they stalked the great white tail buck.

My father loves cherry pies.
I don't understand why, they have a bitter sour taste to me.

I am him though.
At times I find myself sitting a particular way, with my feet crossed stretching my ankles. It makes me think of him. However, it may not be hereditary, could simply be a subconscious memory manifesting in me, from watching him do it so many times when I was a child. Now I see my own son Olin with the same mannerism. Oskar often displays another trait I have picked up from my dad, standing with his hands behind his back, wrist in hand.

Genetic or learned, what resonates with me is the continuation.
Memories, both ancestral and experienced, are passed along.
Cherry pies must be an acquired taste, coming later in life.
I won't be surprised to find them pleasing some day.

Taste is fascinating to me.
I try to pin point my family's origins by what appeals to me.
Certain flavors and spices, or a preference for particular colors, even my response to the weather. I take note of subjective details in my life, always forming a picture of greater clarity. Then, I will stumble across a place that is known for one of the things I favor and it all makes sense. Instantly, a bond through time is apparent and I find the realization comforting.

Tastes are more than just preferences, they become a record, holding the evidence of a previous place and time. Something I can use as a tool to connect with those earlier moments, making me more complete, part of a larger whole.

For my sons, raised in our home modeled around these tastes from ancestors still alive within me and my wife, a symbiotic relationship is established creating an inner balance.

A clay tile roof, hand troweled stucco, vine covered arbors layer a space with reminders, a sense of grounding, a familiar feeling, a place of belonging. My son's senses come looking for relief, our home provides them refuge.

The house I grew up in was a three bedroom house. When my third sister came along, I shared a bedroom with her. Then one day, my father built a partition wall through the middle of their larger bedroom, for me and my oldest sister to each take half. Seven by twelve feet, eighty four square feet. The tightness of the furnishings, a bed, dresser, desk and closet, was very appealing to me. Everything had its place. The highlight of the room was a window at the foot of my bed, a window to the world, filtered by our back yard. The summer sun setting at bedtime filled my room with shadows, sycamore leaves whispering to a gentle breeze.

So much of my childhood was in that room. I would be someone very different without that place. My two youngest sisters shared a room and as they grew older, their protests did not go unnoticed. Their memories of childhood are a different home than mine. My home is dominated by personal space. Moments are shared, but experiences are individualized. Each person treasures different memories from every moment, shaping the perception of every space, to be uniquely their own. A childhood with a private bedroom is a home within a home.

When I designed bedrooms for our children, I based them on my childhood bedroom, but improved. In addition to a window on the world, there is a window to the sky, in a vaulted ceiling. The walls, in a circular plan, lean out. Intentionally keeping the floor area small, just over a hundred square feet, the walls and ceiling open the space up to their imagination.

With all of the maneuvers however, what seems to matter most is not the room defined, but what children bring to the room. Recently our son said, reflecting on why he likes his bedroom, "Everything in here is a memory, like this bird nest is a memory of Grandpa's house."

A room to house a collection of memories.

As a child at home, we played outdoors.
Building tree houses, club houses, snow forts.

But, play at Gra's was indoors, under the orange vinyl chairs.

My clearest memories are times spent with my middle sister, talking into a tape recorder, shyness subdued by the visual barrier of the chair back and seat. Talking silly, making up songs, those chairs provided confidence to perform.

There was always a desire to perform.
Just never the nerve to do so in front of an audience.
A child's stomach is better suited for peanut butter and jelly sandwiches, than butterflies. As an adult, I find myself trying to catch those butterflies, to keep my stomach young.

Maybe as adults, we need fewer orange vinyl chairs.
More open space.
Where we can be exposed, for the world to see.
To help us remember what it feels like to be a child.

Somewhere along the way of growing up, we forget how to talk silly, make up songs, laugh. Adult life is serious, singing by the lyrics, nervous laughter. If you are lucky, children come along twice in life, as your own and then again as grandchildren, to remind us that life's energy is found in greater concentrations within a child's body, overflowing at the source.

But, what if my sister and I never had orange vinyl chairs?
Would we have overcome our stage fright?
Or would we be repressed?

They say orange fish (so called goldfish) grow to the size of their bowl. I think humans do too. If not to the space defined beneath the orange vinyl chairs, then to the space devoid of them. It is not the room that shapes our growth. Growth happens for its own reasons, expanding to fill whatever room we find ourselves in.

Maybe as adults, we need more orange vinyl chairs.
Less open space.
Where we can be contained, to develop slower.
To help us become more aware of what surrounds us.

Maybe not.
We had the chairs and things played out. But, without them something else would have played the role. The human mind is resourceful, certainly the imaginative energy of a child's.

Today those two chairs reside in my sister's house.

And, seeing people sit in them seems odd. The chair in my mind is the gray felt netting stretched beneath the seat, between lacquered spindles tapered down to brass sleeved caps pressing into the carpeted floor. The use of the chair was always the space defined by the four legs or divided by the plane of the vinyl back pulled tight by heavy brass tacks. The space above, enclosed by the arms, was only occupied at times of family gatherings, grown-up talk.

My sister's house has wood floors, harder on the knees of a crouching child. They also sit along an accent wall, not recess corners as in Gra's house. Not surprisingly, her kids are never found hiding under them. Those orange vinyl chairs have been reduced to their designer's original intention of formal sitting, grown-up talk.

I don't think her kids will suffer though.

The only significance in the chairs is the sentimental memories of a brother and sister playing at their grandmother's house.

Not as any butterfly tamers or fish containers.

nëwi-tënti-hëna

Imagine space is circular.
Mathematicians and Physicists may argue it is dimensional, even
with parallel universes. But show me life that exists in the first
or second dimension and I may be convinced of the existence
of a fourth or fifth variety. What we inhabit, so called three
dimensional space, is no more defined by an x, y, or z axis than
by time. Space is space, no matter how humans slice it.

For me, it is a matter of perspective, or more precisely scale.

From our perspective, space is shared with birds and trees. Naturally, things at this scale hold significance for us. Cutting down a tree for a house, displacing a bird's nest is a real act. Something that deserves reverence and gratitude for their upheaval and sacrifice in the name of our own selfish pursuits.

But, how much thought is given to the plight of a microbe, displaced by a cleanser poured down the kitchen drain?
Or, colliding galaxies, bringing an end to myriads of stars?
When perspective is altered by scale, things are very different.

Reducing down to the size of a microbe, then further to the vacuum of space that exists between the smallest of life's building blocks, is the very core of space. Here, without form to reference decreasing size or pace of movement, neither scale nor time exists.

Suddenly, out of nothingness, nearly invisible at first glance, tiny dots begin to emerge. Not sure if they are truly seen or imagined, moving in closer, they turn out to be points of light, stars at the outer edges of our universe.

Imagine if every gene, of every being, contained the universe within the vacuum of each microbe. Not as a genetic tracer of evolution's recorded information, but as the universe itself.

When space is circular, distance between galaxies is no more than a gap of space between synaptic neurons within the brain. The vast scale of stars is the scale of microbes, simultaneous. For the first humans, this was their perspective, circular space.

In the modern era, circular perspective is lost.
Space is sectioned, dimensioned, linear.
Universal truths and ancient knowledge are little respected.
For me, early humans are not that distant, in space or time,
when taken in perspective of the planet's entire existence.

Growing up in central Ohio, one of my first field trips in grade
school was to Serpent Mound. The earthwork's origin and
purpose was uncertain, but for me, the symbolism was the real
mystery. A snake swallowing an egg. Birth and death unified
as one, the eternal return. A long body, undulating back and
forth like a meandering river or wave pattern, ties the head to an
equally sized ovoid spiraling tail. The egg paired with this
decreasing spiral, the circular scale of space and time, without
beginning or end, life becomes here and now, in the moment.

Maybe not. But, inspiration like this never ceases. Sometimes,
inspiration can lead to a new perspective. Recently, my sons
and I were in a canoe drifting along the current of a stream.
Trying to paddle our way back upstream, it occurred to me, that
the water moves slower along the edges, where the stream
meets the land. This realization came quite easily in the doing.
The Adena must have known this too and a connection was
made to them through this insight from the doing. I catch
myself seeking out these proven ways, to gain perspective.

Supported in the center by four horizontal beams atop posts,
the pitched roof of the Adena wigwam spanned downward to
walls leaning out, which were constructed of paired posts
woven with horizontal lath and arranged in a circular plan.

One summer vacation my family visited our nation's capital. The usual stops, Lincoln Memorial, Washington Monument… The ground had just broken on Maya Lin's memorial, but I don't recall visiting the site. What I do recall though, is my first formative memory of an architectural element – the East Wing for the National Gallery by I.M. Pei. As we approached the front steps off Fourth Street, I asked my mom if I could go over to the towering wall to the right of the entrance. I remember thinking that maybe people weren't suppose to get close to it, as I stepped off the pavement onto the grass lawn. But, I was going to anyway, I was drawn in. I couldn't resist touching the narrowing edge, to see for myself if it was real or an illusion. The juxtaposition of such a massive wall, soaring to great heights, against a stark simplicity of monolithic stone brought to a crisply charged fold, an edge to fit within the palm of a fourteen year old hand.

The result of a triangular floor plan, defined by the radical imposition of Pennsylvania Avenue onto the Mall's regular grid, it was an urban planning move that would make any student of architecture skew with excitement. Well, Mr. Pei could not resist either and went on to create a gesture that would have me questioning architecture for the first time in my life.

But I hadn't seen anything yet. The following summer, my parents took us to see the national parks on the other side of the Mississippi. Our first stop was the gateway to the west, the St. Louis arch by Eero Saarinen. A poetic gesture of pure mathematics, an inverted parabola, also triangular in section, but with a delicate tapering from its base up to its central peak, suspended effortless in the heavens above. Again, I couldn't resist, I was drawn to the interior edge, vaulting downward to meet the ground. Like a magnetic force, I was pulled in, to touch the panelized seam with my own hands and then to take in the dizzying view upward and across to the other side.

A second architectural moment distinctively marked in my memory, realization that man-made structures could be more than a rectilinear box, even something beautiful when their lines are gently rounded. However, this is not all I took away from my first encounter with Mr. Saarinen. Wondering around in the visitor's center submerged below ground, I was fascinated by the massive poured concrete embankments at the entries between the two legs of the arch. The most appropriate expression of Brutalism I would ever see, the sloping surfaces relegated to the subterranean world, simultaneously anchored and counter-balanced the weightless arch in the sky above.

It wasn't until several years later, returning to Washington D.C. that I began to comprehend the significance of the ground plane for a structure. Maya Lin's memorial was complete and I was now at an age more capable of appreciating the nuance of her gesture. A gentle reveal in the land, reverent to the earth as much as to the subject of the commission. A massive wall, horizontally expansive, yet again I was drawn to its central fold, of a human scale. A desire to reach out and touch this interior recess, the heart of these shifting planes. This architecture was not placed atop the landscape, it was the landscape, physically and metaphysically. Architecture was no longer an additive construct. For me, it became a reductive grounding.
A density, a gravitation, a sediment.

Architecture was something residing in the essence.
The edifice simply provided a subtle insight in.

Growing up as a child wanting to be an architect, I never met one, so there wasn't even an image in my mind of what they were like. The first one I learned of was Frank Lloyd Wright. And, by the time I went off to school to study architecture, Wright had become the standard by which I measured everything. It wasn't long before a classmate and I took a road trip one weekend, four hours east to the site of his most acclaimed masterpiece, Fallingwater.

Because we were students, setting off without calling ahead, nor a map, once we found our way, the entrance drive was locked for the night. Refusing to be deterred, we backtracked down the road, to where it crossed a small creek. Surely this must be Bear Run, the infamous creek that ran through the Kaufman's summer house. Parking the car alongside the road, we began walking up the creek anxious to see the house emerge from the woods. It was a greeting far better than a guided tour down the drive. Our first glimpse, the classic view, looking up at the water cascading over the bluff with his cantilevering terraces inspiring awe and complete humility. We were mere students in the presence of true genius.

All of his theories I had read paled in comparison to the immediacy and clarity of understanding that came from inhabiting the space he created. In that moment, Mr. Wright taught me the power of details. Not just the delicacy of scale, focusing attention on an exquisitely crafted joint or the significance of visual landmarks establishing a reference to navigate his endless sequence of unfolding space. No, what resonated most for me was the unity. The space was held together by the details, literally and metaphorically. Not simply a repetition of iconographic branding, carried mindlessly throughout the house, in every turn and alcove recess. His talent was far more than that. Every room, every transition, every material was an opportunity to elevate the essence of the home, evolving a deeper level of meaning from the last. As much as he wanted his architecture to express the character of its inhabitants, the details were his signature, unmistakable. Fallingwater belonged to no one except the heavy hand of Frank Lloyd Wright.

Architectural history lectures were always held in a darkened room at eight in the morning, a true test of will to keep eyes open while sitting perfectly still and coming off multiple nights at work in studio, a cruel device deployed to weed out the uncommitted in the first quarter of the architecture program. This was the setting of my first exposure to Antonio Gaudí. The first slide I saw was of a colonnaded pathway he created into the hillside of Park Güell. It seemed so natural, so simple, so clear. Why hadn't this been done before? More importantly, why hadn't everyone followed? Regardless of others, at this moment there was no doubt I knew where I was going.

His work broke from all of the rules, guided by intuition, not by the limitations of regimented geometries, he understood the gravity of details and somehow managed to redefine them. Somewhere between a hand drawn sketch and a drafted hard line drawing, a quality that reflects its author is lost. Preserving that original intent, much closer to the source and therefore more pure in the impact, he honed his senses to guide his decisions, trusting what felt right.

Things that need explained to be understood do not interest me as much as things the body and soul respond to innately. My own home became a place to study this language, to live with it and to comprehend its nuance on architectural space. It is a matter of human perception, constructed thresholds. Doing so, I have come to realize the role of an architect is to define.

Define the intent.
Define the means.
Define the limits.

Then to surround oneself with the finest craftsmen, step back and let them do their thing. It is the broad strokes of an architect that truly define the character of a space. The creative idea, the flow of the composition, the implications of the elements. Artisans in tune will perceive these overtones and accentuate them in their work. Understand your role and trust their experience, micromanaging never produced anything of lasting value. Architecture is a collaborative art.

In my own bathroom, the division line between tile and plaster was conceived by the gesture of my hand, drawn on the walls. Areas of concentration and void, setting the feel of the room.

By doing so, ideas in my head, specific to me, were transferred directly to the walls, imbuing them with me. It is a small thing, not on the surface, just below it, tapping into the subconscious, where architectural space emerges.

Form can not be denied.

The original language, form is primary.
Defining material, texture, even space.
In the case of an architect, a sincere understanding is necessary
to master. Ignorance of how it speaks is negligence.

At first glance, a Venetian gondola appears symmetrical.
Yet, why does it have a straight course when the gondolier's oar
is always on one side? The haul has a subtle asymmetrical bias
to the right, balanced by rowing to the left.

Just as one holds a hand above their eyes in bright sunlight or
cups a hand behind their ear in a noisy room, gesture in form
activates space in a perceptible way, physically, but also
metaphysically.

In undergraduate school, I was fascinated by how form operated, the techniques employed to make it more persuasive, the degree of influence it had on space. I studied it everywhere. At that time, print advertising for the clothing industry was at the cutting edge. Architecture wasn't even a distant second. The Spring and Fall issues of monthly fashion magazines, Bazaar, Elle, Vogue routinely had 700, 800, 900 pages. Brilliant photographers, such as Sheila Metzner, Ellen von Unwerth, Sante d'Orazio, were given freedom by advertisers to elevate images to a work of art. Even their subjects were raised to the status of Supermodel, known simply by their first names. The very clothing they were commissioned to market was overpowered. I rarely took note of a garment's label, much less the name of the designer. For me, the printed page taught lessons on form.

Composition, framing, asymmetry, juxtaposition, proportion, volume, weight, balance, rhythm, tension, gesture, profile, void, lighting, shading, color, texture… above all else, stood beauty. That elusive quality that inspires, within the realm of poetry, the foundation on which nature herself is bound.

What is form without beauty?
In today's times, beauty is a negative word. Pretentious.
That might be, but those who think so are not being honest. Beauty is simply a matter of motivation. That's its given role, nothing more. And yet, this principle underlies everything.

Martin Skalski, the transportation design professor in the Industrial Design program at Pratt, taught me everything on the subject I longed for in undergraduate school but couldn't seem to find. He approached the issue of form head on, no apologies for superficiality or moral vacancies. It was simply a matter of manipulation, visual effect, coercion. Learning how to see and then refine. Taken on its own merits, within that context, it is a foundation necessary for every designer.

The allure of form is envelopment.

Visceral recesses, empty, gravitating toward silent equilibrium, will attract. Comfort, filling a concavity or external fold, balanced, instinctual kineticism. Density, measured medium.

Villa Vuoto was designed with varying radii spiraling in plan, simplistic geometry to instill a solidity and bold definition at corner transitions, to avoid arbitrary non-mathematic freeform.

Straight linear segments leaning in vertical section, maintained clarity and elegance of oblique conical interior surfaces and the hyperboloidal exterior surfaces from inverted stacked rooms.

Form is metaphor, the universal mode of communication. Anatomic vocabulary based on the human condition is more immediate, but rarely can Mother Nature be outdone. Often a simple movement grounded in the study of proportional mass and spatial angularity at corner transitions is the best place to practice its influences. Understanding comes from dedication.

The first time I experienced Richard Serra's Torqued Ellipses was his 1998 show at The Contemporary in Los Angeles. Dense volumes with graceful contortions and slender vertical slots inviting me in. The thickness of the steel (two inches) and the warm colors of the rust were hard to resist touching. Their impact on me was immediate, sensory overload. Circular spaces defined by walls leaning away and toward. It wasn't the first time I had occupied space in this configuration, but it certainly was the most memorable.

The intimacy of the scale was powerful, relating to an individual. Even with so many of them collected together in such a public venue, it was difficult to think of them as anything but a private space. Other visitors standing within them at the same time felt like an intrusion. With all of them packed into this warehouse style interior, it was as if I was walking through Serra's studio. Even better, Serra was there that day, incognito, watching the people move through his work and seeing their responses to the spaces. I approached him to compliment his pieces and to ask some logistic questions on their fabrication. He was pleased to tell me of his process for modeling them and how he used an eastern water technique to bend them. The chance meeting was the perfect pairing for my first encounter with his ellipses.

Nearly a decade later, I went to Serra's forty year retrospective at MoMA in New York. One of the ellipses that I saw back in Los Angeles was outside in the sculpture garden. It was the first time I had experienced a piece of art in two different settings, a chance to explore the degree of influence surroundings have on an object. It couldn't have been a better test case, nearly polar opposite: a single ellipse, open to the sky outdoors and located on the east coast. The allure of the surface was still there, but less so. And the density was diminished too, by the cavernous space of the towering buildings on the four sides of the garden. The sense of intimacy was lost and very difficult for me to get into, only fleeting moments. The energy of the city created a setting that was ultimately overpowering. It was a piece on display in a show, not a space to inhabit within a series of studies.

All was not lost though. Serra had made three new pieces. Torqued Torus Inversion, was a pair of ellipses set side by side, one with a slotted entry hovering overhead and the other receding away. Unlike his earlier ellipses that had walls with a straight sectional profile, these were convex from the interior. The difference was significant. Rather than a space that envelopes, grounding me with an awareness of the weight of these skins, the slight belly of the walls in these new ellipses, with their top and bottom edges pulling away, made the density dissolve. Weightless.

Serra had transformed the inherent physical properties of steel by the gesture of its form. The actual weight of the steel hadn't changed, but the perceptual effect on the senses had. No longer did these pieces impress with their mass, the enormity of their undertaking. They had become transcendent into the realm of the sublime. Without a change to the decoration of their surface, dimensional scale or qualities of the material, he was able to play within the confines of the subconscious mind, using form to manipulate effects beyond the physical. It was a single move, bending the surface with two perpendicular opposing arcs when previously only one.

Frank Gehry had done the same thing with Bilbao. But his effect was achieved by the surfacing material more than the compounded curves. Before Bilbao, museums were designed to instill solidity, the illusion of importance. Gehry covered the new Guggenheim with thin sheet metal shingles, oil cans and all, to the point where critics drew attention to the noise they created when the wind blew. In contrast, Richard Meier during the same time period was undertaking his masterwork, the Getty Museum on the west coast and went to great lengths to bring a specific type of Italian stone half way around the world to cement its grandeur. But, Gehry changed all of that in a single building. With the help of sensuous forms, his titanium skin was elevated, transporting the material beyond preconceived associations and into a new definition.

In kind, Serra's ellipses had now done it, but with an economy of gesture. A reduction to the essence of metaphysical form.

After moving to Pittsburgh from Los Angeles,
I discovered a museum on the north side unlike any other.
One dedicated to installation art, pushing toward architecture,
in the sense, the artists create a transformative space.

Yoshihiro Suda's work was one of the first I experienced.
When I entered his room, it looked empty, thinking it was not part of the show I moved on to the next room. But, I distinctly remember thinking this museum was so unique and a great venue for experimenting artists, because it wasn't the typical white sterile box hermetically sealed, this museum breathed. Although it had brick walls and squeaky wood floors, remnants of an earlier factory, it was the occasional weed growing up through a crack that made it seem as if anything was possible in this museum. A small thing, but a very powerful detail.

But this weed, in this room, was not thriving in a museum that seemed to leave such things unattended. It was placed their by the artist and that was his only installation into the space. With that single minimal gesture, he achieved his effect and in a way that cemented for me the power of small moves operating in the realm of a secondary forum. Not a primary arena where things are obviously presented as the main attraction, set on a pedestal and framed, as if to say this is what you are to look at, bringing with it all of the context and precedent of an establishment. No, this background medium is understated, intended to operate directly on the senses bypassing the conscious mind. And, in that format, the effect is much quicker, a visceral response, the kind of thing that happens with a first impression. One often can't put a finger on it, but the feeling stays with you. Resonating on a deeper level, these feelings become lasting memories and set the atmosphere for all the other elements that operate on the surface.

Rolf Julius experiments within the same dimension, but with a different device, the ears. Pitch and volume are modulated to sit at the edge of conscious awareness. In this case, the sounds of birds chirping emanates from crevices in stones walls of an outdoor garden, the entrance to the museum. Again, one walks by thinking nothing more than a few birds must be nearby, as if one was walking into an aviary. But the effect is undeniable. Everyone perceives it and their impression of the space is influenced by it, even though the reason and cause might go unnoticed.

James Turrell takes it a little further. In one of his permanent installations into the museum, he uses the medium of light to play on the subconscious mind, but he is upfront about it. Entering a darkened room, feeling your way to a seat, the stage is set where you expect to see something. You are looking for his piece and it takes a few minutes to find it. The light projected on the wall in front of you is so dim, that your eyes need to adjust before you begin to see it. At least you think you see it, but as time passes you begin to think maybe not. You become unsure. There is a faint spot visible, but it is difficult to determine if it is something in the room or in your eyes, much like the spots visible after looking at a light bulb. Boundary is blurred between you and your surroundings.

The Mattress Factory Museum forever shaped my view on architecture, making clear where its true strength lies. Even more, the museum has become a standard from which I measure my own work and a place I can return to frequently, tuning my subconscious sensibilities.

Keeping the senses sharp is the life blood of an architect.
And one has to continually work at it, selectively exposing oneself to particular environments, to improve their tool set.

Manfred Honeck's debut as the new music director of the Pittsburgh Symphony was one such event. My wife and I were sitting in the last row of the balcony, my favorite place to sit. On the second piece, a prelude written by a Russian composer, something happened reminiscent of these experimental artists.

Mr. Honeck is a soft spoken man. So much so, watching an interview of him almost becomes a strain to comprehend his words through his whispers tainted by an Austrian accent. Before this performance, I thought it just an oddity, but on the last few bars of this piece, it all became apparent.

A musical phrase repeated to conclude the movement and as conductor, Mr. Honeck brought the volume down progressively with each play. To the point on the last rendition, I could not tell if the sound was coming from the instruments or they had fallen silent to the gentle and slowing motion of his baton. From the last row of the auditorium, the faintest of notes do not always carry. And in this case, they may not have. All that I might have heard was the sound of the previous bars still ringing in my head. I listened intently holding my breath, focusing my attention, as hard as I tried I couldn't be certain. Those last few notes ventured into the roots of the mind, where perception is suspended between the internal and the external.

La Jetée, a short film by Chris Marker takes this duality into a medium at the heart of architectural space. A story of explorers able to travel back through time, by probing the depths and power of emotional memory. Through the mind places are visited, not replayed as a past memory, but using the catalog of information to tap into an earlier moment. Division between personal experiences and shared moments becomes unclear, calling into question the location of the subconscious and its role linking the two. Space is cerebral, permeating without limit.

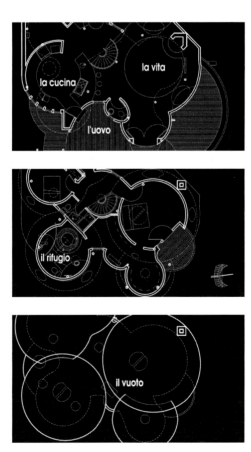

435

i cinque punti di architettura:

l'uovo
shelter, warmth, shade… a sense of safety and comfort.
An external envelope, for protection from the natural elements.

la vita
living, laughing, conversing… the open part of a home.
A place to entertain guests and grow social relationships.

la cucina
cook, dine, bond… the source of nourishment.
A fire and table, for family to gather around and share.

il rifugio
recline, rest, rejuvenate… a private suite.
A familiar place, to escape the stresses in daily life.

il vuoto
void, śūnyatā, nothingness… the source of creativity.
A personal space for reflection and giving thanks.

In undergraduate school at Ohio State, our studio was reprimanded for what was called a 'shanty town'. Sheets of chipboard and foamcore pinned to cantilevering balsa and basswood sticks, enclosing the drafting tables of naive students eager to inhabit their own designs. But the administration, just as eager to bring potential donors through the studios, wanted first impressions of an idea foundry, not a slum settlement.

Equally emphasized though, was focus on 'affordable housing' design for low income and homeless found in urban centers. The recent population shift, with a majority of people now living in cities, has one out of three urban dwellers living in shanty towns, nearly a billion people. These settlements on the edge of civilization, often lack urban planning, formal streets, sanitation networks, electricity or police, medical, and fire fighting services. What they do offer is a knowledge base for sustainable living, efficient footprints, low energy usage, reclaimed materials, community centered, handmade by the inhabitants, and the maximization of existing topography. Occupying the leftover spaces, squatters are the largest builders of housing in the world, mixing more concrete, laying more brick than any commercial developer or national government.

A house is more than a luxury, it is necessary for survival.
When society does not provide enough, ingenuity steps in.

Essential needs are met, beginning with the external elements, a roof overhead and walls to enclose, followed by a proxemic layering of space, from the place defined by social interaction down to a private spot for personal reflection or meditation.

Form follows need.

To escape the heat of the day and the cold of the night, merchants traveling the desert trade routes would put up high ceiling tents, covering the sand and sides with rich carpets, then light them with spectacular pierced bronze lanterns. Nomadic people, they carried only the essentials. Practicality is the great reductionist, quickly identifying frivolity. Decorations such as these served more than a wind break and comfort extended beyond the physical body or pleasures of the eye. The vastness of the desert can overwhelm the mind. Merely a grain in a sea of sand, these travelers pitched ceilings and walls so they could define their space, rather than be defined by it.

What is this need for a lamp post at night?
To see where we go in hurry or flight?
No… it is to mask our fear with light
of truth hidden in stars only visible at night.

Nature's unknowns are too much for many. Separation at a safe distance is often provided by muted boxes, a vocabulary foreign to the universe, to give credence we are beyond it. What little exposure we allow ourselves is carefully controlled through shaded windows and closed doors.

My graduate thesis studied the affects of architectural form and space on people. Installations tested visual perception and proxemic variations. Since that time, in my professional practice, I have come to realize the space architectural form defines is personal, perceived differently by every person. Intimate within the space of a home.

Daily life is filled with feelings, intuition, premonition. And yet, when a friend asks what you have done today, responses rarely include 'I looked at the sun's reflection in the window or rain drops running down a windowpane.' Solitude can sometimes bring intense moments of fullness. It's all these little things, often too personal to share, that define a person.

Consciously, most of these moments are forgotten. Every once in a while though, one will resonate on some level and become a memory lasting a lifetime. Life is not a series of sunsets, it is a particular sunrise, taken in at a specific time. In the end, these intimate moments are the great driving force behind motivations, our doings, even if we are not aware.

Days are filled making memories from moments, it is natural. The act of doing so, the act of creating, is so fundamental to existence, the desire to create externally is merely a reflection. Creating a home is no different. An intimate act, in the doing, the manifestation of walls and a roof are simply a housing. When we vacate the walls, home goes with us, as a memory.

Our primary home is our being, this is where we live our lives. The world around us is filtered by it and when that world is brought into our mind as a memory, our being distorts it, shapes it, makes it our own. When overwhelmed by a world with such vastness of space, distortions become a survival mechanism for the mind, to find relief.

We never regain the level of security, comfort, connection as in the prenatal abyss, though we never stop trying. Further back, cravings originating from long lost ancestral habits can never be fully quenched. And the original loss, a return to the source of creation is impossible in the flesh. Rather, we are sentenced to a lifetime of searching and home becomes a substitute, temporary attempt to fulfill longings.

The beholder beckons to their home and vacancies in their being shape the space they inhabit, a palimpsest of memories. And it's in the context of this triangle that architecture is made, distortions of perception the mind creates filling voids.

Solace can only be found within the space of a home, by our own doing. An architect has no place in the matter.

510

The day was not intended to be a special day beyond any other. But as it turned out, it was one that changed my perspective irreversibly from that moment forward. I was researching sliding stones of Death Valley and made a general word search on the internet for images, when the results page popped up an unrelated photograph.

A young child crawling to a UN food camp nearly a mile away is head down on the ground, resting nearly an hour, to build up the energy to continue. Just beyond a vulture stands waiting.

As a father of two children, my first thought was what kind of world do we live in, where a child is left to fend for themselves at such a helpless age. Looking at the vulture preying over the child, put the human race right back into the animal kingdom. Before that day, I lived in a world where humans were at the top of the food chain. Our babies at least had civilization to protect them. That was the primary reason we banded together in the first place, building homes tightly clustered behind walls, to separate ourselves from the beasts.

Exactly three weeks earlier, I watched a film by Cao Fei at the Carnegie International. It was a piece about the lives and dreams of factory workers making light bulbs in China. The screening was set in a noisy stair hall, where the voices of school children touring the exhibition drowned out the soundtrack as they shuffled by. I found it an interesting commentary on two societies bound by economic forces, one's existence surviving on the insatiable consumerism of the other. And yet, the ignorance and indifference these school children paid to a film documenting this endless mass of people, who sacrifice their dreams for a life in their world, was emblematic of the disconnect that exists between these two cultures. It crushed my belief in the value of a single life. If a billion people can go unnoticed, what chance does a single life have to find fulfillment? If there is no chance, what's the point?

In Mr. Rogers' Neighborhood, assembly line workers were special. Each and every one of them. In the entire world, there is no one else just like you. That might be true, but what is the meaning of a life when the numbers become so large that individuals are lost in the madness and dreams are abandoned?

Cynicism toward the human race was inevitable.
I guess it was always there for me, but the timing of these two experiences made it crystal clear. I always felt uncomfortable living at the top of the food chain. In my mind, the human elitism of western culture is a setback, not an accomplishment. Setting ourselves apart from the other life forms had a subtle, but profound implication on our perspective.

Numbness to our surroundings.

This is primarily why I forced myself to watch the beheading of Eugene Armstrong by a man on a crusade of terror against America. An image that will haunt me forever, of an act that no one should be subjected to witness. But, to live my life without facing the ugliness that exists to afford my lifestyle, would perpetuate the numbness in me.

Politics aside, it was an act of barbarism, the horrors of which have no justifiable reason in modern day life. Denial is almost a natural defense mechanism, to preserve one's sanity in an insane world. However, the same act is depicted in American cinema far too often and the entertainment thrill is only possible by numbness toward the barbaric nature.

It is widespread, permeating every facet of society.
But, it is on the subtle level that carries the greatest threat.

Recently, I noticed a curious development in the road construction for the Pennsylvania Turnpike where it crosses the Allegheny River. Typically, rolling hills in the path of motorists are cut into, to minimize elevation change, making transport safer and easier. Often those cuts exposed bedrock within the hills that weep groundwater during Spring rains and collect ice sickles during Winter months. Most people think nothing of it as they hurry past to their destination. Here, at the foothills of the Appalachian Mountains, the exposed bedrock is layered sediment, horizontal bands of shale and sandstone with the occasional coal seam adding a rich black shade. On this particular stretch of roadway, adding more lanes resulted in steeper cuts, which required a wall to stabilize the hillside. Retaining walls are nothing new, but this one scored lines into sprayed on concrete to simulate the horizontal banding of these sedimentary rocks common to southwestern Pennsylvania.

This marked a change in society's perspective. The exposed bedrock, a byproduct of the high speed roadway, was no longer just a consequence but now had become nostalgia.
Society's numbness toward transfiguration of the natural landscape enabled a sentimentality to emerge. A fondness for a new aesthetic based on the remnants of human indifference.

why?

As a student, this question dominated architectural discourse. No wonder, much of life's existential ideas center on the same. Any good theory must certainly address this question and the end product needs to be a physical manifestation of the answer. But it seemed, in practice, so many did not. Or worse, an aesthetic bias drove the theory.

In any event, what I quickly learned was the importance placed on a parti in the architectural profession. That foundation still weighs heavily on me and to a large extent is the reason for this writing, a declaration of the ideas behind my work.

Architecture, as in all of the arts, involves the subjective. Academically, to avoid this issue of taste, a creative idea is not judged on its seductive nature. Rather, theory enters to apply a scientific means of debate and as a measure of successfulness.

Jeffrey Kipnis introduced me to architectural theory. His critique of student work cut straight to the heart of the issue, often from an angle unexpected, but always with such clarity and precision of description, the obviousness seemed irrefutable and alternate readings became flat out irrelevant. His undergraduate studio at Ohio State University always had me questioning, eventually formulating my own test: a theory well constructed can be used as a set of assembly instructions, by independent practitioners, to arrive at the same aesthetic.

I would argue this is rarely achieved. Yet, this is the standard I set for myself. Eventually I found, ideas not so easily spoken, intuitive based, translated into the material much easier. Through a visual vocabulary based on visceral response, conscious theory was supplanted by subconscious awareness.

Your initial, diagrammatic response to a design problem is generally bold, abstract with regard to programmatic limits, and of sculptural interest.

Such was the commentary of one of my early design professors. Where I struggled was the application of 'why?', how to translate the idea into form. In graduate school, I began to find out, but also came to realize I was studying the wrong question.

As a child, a different question dominated everyday life. When told by parents, 'No you can not', kids ask, 'why not?' Now as a parent myself, it is clear, the reasons why not are impositions placed on life by society, closing minds, reducing human potential, stifling creativity.

Deborah Gans cemented the importance of this question. Her classes and the opportunity to work alongside in her practice defined my graduate development at Pratt Institute. In no other architect have I witnessed as much passion for the integrity of the work and her example has left me with the energy and curiosity of a child, never accepting status quo. Not a day goes by in my practice that I don't apply her lesson.

Some of mankind's greatest achievements come from those who asked 'why not?', ignoring those who explained why not. As an architect, solutions come quickest for me when 'givens' are thrown out the window. Every convention is questioned, 'how did this come to be this way?', 'can it be another way?' Certain things prove their value, the reasons for their current configuration make sense, so they stay. Others are less so, their existence appear arbitrary and consequently get scrutinized.

Some time ago, irritated by a tag on my undershirt that itched my neck, it occurred to me to wear the shirt inside out. Unexpected, was an increase in comfort, beyond the tag issue. The shirt seams were no longer against my skin, a small detail, but perceivable. The kind of difference felt from a tailored suit. It wasn't long and I was wearing my socks inside out too.

When my youngest son Olin began dressing himself, his shirt would often end up inside out. But then, it was not uncommon for his pants to be on backwards or socks not match.

weep holes
thermal breaks
expansion joints

Concrete cracks.
It is in the nature of the material to crack, inherent to the physical properties of the curing and moisture levels.

Most people do not like cracks, believe them to be imperfect.
Most architects do not like them either, a line too organic, shaped like a tree branch or lightning bolt, a visual aesthetic that rarely compliments Cartesian grids or Euclidean cubes. Actually, it comes down to a control issue. Architects are anal over control and every application of every material must perform as planned, which is their objection to cracks. It is the reason they created control joints, to tell the crack where to go.

I prefer to let cracks go where they like, in their own time.
They provide an insight that can not be heard without listening.
To become a true master of building materials, one must not force a preconceived idea upon them, but rather look to the material to understand its inherent properties and the way it responds to different conditions. Continuously expanding and contracting, the crack is a barometer of atmospheric conditions, humidity, temperature. Materials are never static, nor are they intended for assembling some romanticized image, frozen in time. Every material is in a constant state of change, either growing or decaying, at different rates. True architecture understands this principle and celebrates it through the design. A floor without cracks is sterile, without life, incomplete.

Listen to the cracks.

Ornamentation is a commentary on a particular age. An ogee coupled with a cavetto for visual effect, manipulating light to define form, is also a statement of style, a reference, homage. For me, it has always represented an inferior quality of work. Trim is conventionally used to hide unfinished edges, allowing materials to be assembled by less skilled tradesmen, with the finish trimwork covering all the rough handling done for the sake of speed and cost efficiencies. For trim to be anything more, it needs to be historically accurate. Then it is no longer a synthetic imitation, but becomes something meaningful, eliciting a visceral response genuine to the intent of the profile.

I never envisioned Villa Vuoto with trim. Not because crown molding or base boards would contradict the design aesthetic, but for a more fundamental reason – a mousetrap.

For me, interest is usually found at the edges, in the corners. Attention to detail is not always a measure of accuracy or cleanliness. A single brushstroke by a seasoned calligrapher can be rough at the edges, but still perfectly true to the intent. How edges are handled speaks to the work as a whole. When the design process begins, my first marks are generally bold, containing an energy or feeling that I try not to loose in subsequent refinements. Architecture is the manifestation of the idea, as my grandfather would say, 'do it right'.

However, most people prefer clean edges, precisely trimmed. This tendency says more about people than the architecture. The world is not a neat and tidy place, things happen with less clarity, slightly out of focus.

So the walls of our home are plastered right down to the floor. In some cases a smudge is found on the concrete, maybe in a tight corner, but for me, this is a more accurate reflection of life.

die mauer im kopf

During the unification of Germany, I read an article about the Berlin Wall, the psychological effects it would have after it came down. This made me curious about the images people hold within their mind of their physical surroundings, more specifically, what in their surroundings create those images.

In studying this relationship, I have found that recording an object by observing it through memory alone leads to an intriguing form of aesthetic analysis, the visual and cognitive ties in a physical form. I began to do this with the places I remembered from when I was growing up, my childhood home, Gra's apartment, Ash Cave. Drawing sketches, beginning with the elements that held vivid memories, followed by supporting details, then finally, the most interesting part for me, the areas that were least clear, difficult to remember, recesses in these childhood places that have now created recesses in my mind.

I often use my undergraduate school shoes as a tool, to keep me humble, recalling the sincerity of focus I had as a student. Or when feeling intimidated, wear dress shoes to find courage.

Objects in a memory work differently. The mind changes these objects, romanticizing those we hold in high regard or exaggerating the horrible things that caused us harm. Extremes are not hard to recall, it is the forgotten things that are more subtle, acting more profoundly on one's being. Although the conscious mind may not remember these things, they are still there, locked away in the subconscious. Getting at them takes time, but they tend to offer the greatest reward.

I begin by tying up loose ends to eliminate any distractions, relax my body, clear my mind, calm my thoughts, still as a rock. From here, I listen, focusing on natural rhythms I sense. Soon my conscious mind begins to loosen, memories flow more freely from the subconscious and fragments start popping up. Carefully, I sketch, trying to mark succinctly without breaking the thread of lucidity. In the end, paper now records a memory, much easier to reference and study.

I take these memory sketches with me when I go back to visit these earlier places or objects. I am always amazed by the level of detail that comes through, things drawn just as I find them. But, I place my attention on the things that are different.
Like a romanticized or dreaded memory, over time, the mind alters reality, so what we take away from a moment is something other than the truth, something particular to us, something more meaningful than what reality could offer.

These distortions, blurred at the edges and relegated to the subconscious are the real truth, what define and differentiate us from everyone else. They are a reflection of our character, priorities, desires, and an examination of them reveals insight into the nuance of a person. For a home to resonate on this level, it comes from here, not an architect, an outsider. As an architect, my greatest service can only be a guide through the process, providing knowledge from my experience and training, not the actual act of defining a home around oneself.

After graduation, I moved to Los Angeles to complete intern requirements before sitting for the licensing exams. I was fortunate to work for the architect considered by many the greatest designer of retail and entertainment architecture in the western world, Jon Jerde, who saw his work as creating the modern town square, place making.

One of the first projects I worked on was an addition to his own home, a cherished stone house designed and built by his architectural mentor. To be honest, I found it odd to find myself working on modifications to his private residence. Maybe this is why it had gone through years of endless design permutations and never realizing one of them. What felt right to Jon, worth doing, could only be drawn by him.

Janice, his wife and also an architect, taught me as much about architecture. My time in her office represents nearly everything I know about courting and fostering the client relationship. However, one of her greatest gifts to me was the use of their home when travels took them away. The brief time spent in their home gave me more insight into Janice and Jon, then all of the design meetings, reviews and studies performed as the routine process in designing a house. A home is one of the most intimate expressions of the mind and spirit. And is therefore, one of the most immediate mediums to learn about a person, by living within their space.

Those days in their home taught me how they saw architecture, sensitivities to material and color, sequencing of rooms, the importance of experience. Every act of daily life unfolded, helping me to understand the true nature of space. In the end, my designs for alterations to their house were never used, but more importantly, the opportunity taught me something far more valuable. Creating a home is a personal matter, best left to the dweller. For a home to provide true relief, it must account for our most intimate needs. Maybe that is why a new house does not feel like ours, until we create something in it, a decoration, a special occasion, a pie. Shaping the house, making it part of us, so our earlier memories feel at home.

有
生
於
无

To design Villa Vuoto, I began with my mind empty, vuoto, open to any possibility. Being originates from non-being, void, nothingness, the source of creativity.

Limitations are defining, they can become excuses or a device. When approached with optimism and preconceived ideas are abandoned, alternatives come to light, often better than the original conception that was complicated by limitation.

The glass shower curtain in our bathroom is my best example. The original idea was to combine the transparency and elegance of a glass enclosure with the qualities of a hanging curtain. After several variations of the glass pieces in shape and size, they were priced to have them cut and tempered. Estimates exceeded the budget for the entire bathroom, so an alternative solution was necessary, if the original idea was to be preserved. Using the limitation of cost as the impetus, I went in the opposite direction, to see what might result. The new goal was to create a glass shower curtain with as little expense possible. Discontinued glass plates from Target, fishing line and some binder clips resulted in a pattern of fish scales and the effect of rippling water from the distortions of the blue mosaic tiles filtering through the circular plates. Metaphors I struggled for earlier, manifested without effort in this direction.

I don't seek them out, but when limitations arise, they do not trouble me, rather I am pleased, knowing that something new is just around the corner. All I need to do is let go of the limitation I am holding on to and head toward the unexpected.

Limitations, the gateway to creativity. Not a wall, but a door with windows, providing an insight and direction for passage. Embrace them, they are milestones to lead the way.

Limitations of the mind are another matter. Precautions must be taken continuously, since they are a natural part of the way our brains process information. Differentiation is a strategy for organizing our thoughts, however, necessity to categorize must be done with an awareness of limitations from stereotypes.

Le Corbusier warned of the detrimental effect a visit to the ruins of Greece could have on a student of architecture. Everything you come in contact with makes an impression. The mind cannot unsee once it has seen. The best strategy for powerful images is avoidance, selective exposure.

So, from an initial intent, I am careful of where I go, what I see, what I do, what I read. The act of selecting what I expose myself to is as much of the creative process for me as the doing. Limiting external influences concentrates the effectiveness of the ones I seek out, enriching and heightening the experience. But before they are taken in, the mind must be cleared, silenced to let go of any past notions that might limit possibilities. Nothingness, where creativity begins and is often found.

I become suspicious when there is a sense of familiarity…
                                    things falling into place.
Aware, I play along
ask no questions, but pursue with intrigue.

As time passes, synchronicities lead the way.
Like a talent, I trust blind intuition
however refinement comes from practice,
                                    so I have become an addict.
I fear an understanding. Fragile and subtle,
to look inside abandons the desired outcome.
An accomplice, there is no option, I simply follow
                                    ends work out.
Naivety protects, providing hallowed passage.

Transcendence
in a pleasure moment. All is answered
inconsequential since questions lose any significance.
I have found the eternal. Bound not by space or time,
                                    circular singularity.
Always there, just below consciousness,
revelation is instinctual.
Captured, within a fetish, the object a portal, to remember.

322

creative energy

Thermal currents adrift, condensing vapors become drops, raining down, returning to the sea. Lifted up again by sunlight, concentrations occur, receiving and releasing, evidence of life.

Ethereal, like any other fluid, imbalance disperse, equalized, neural seepage. Ideas spread outward, to be gathered, shared. Perpetual, thriving because it can, creation is an energy beyond limits, control is futile. Tuning to the ebb and flow, receptive sensitivity, the act of listening, without coercion, touches that which drives the universe.

Networks composed of fluid allow for unrelated elements to become close in proximity. In this context, something interesting happens, pairs pare pear.

It is the convergence that interests me, I make note when it happens in my own mind, identifying time, place, or any context that seems relevant to their formation. On review, patterns emerge, a twittering machine.

The human brain is made up of neurons, one hundred billion. Interconnected, ends of neurons branch out into dendrites, thousands on each, communicating via chemical ions and electrical charges. Possible combinations exceed the number of elementary particles in the universe. Paired relays in parallel with one skipping over a series, creates a signal in repetition, sustaining an impulse over time, relational to the collection of stimuli in unison from all the senses, in that moment a unique composition is differentiated, a thought. Configurations are in constant change, but compositions repeated become familiar as pathways refine from practice, the formation of a memory, eventually passing information along genetically. Increased firings creates a density greater than the surrounding uniformity, perceptible imbalance, bringing those impulses into conscious awareness above the field of disperse firings occurring in the background subconscious. Concentration is consciousness. Densities have a tendency toward equilibrium, thoughts in front of the mind mingle with those in the back. Tethers between leave residues locally measured with those drifting externally. It is when these two are proxemic that a new idea is born.

Children do this intuitively, still believing anything is possible. It is not that they dream up wondrous ideas, but rather provide fertile ground for growth, instinctively processing so much information around them, without preconceived notions. Somewhere between childhood and adolescence, when d is no longer b, children loose that creative spirit. Conventions are encouraged at the sacrifice of insatiable curiosity and divisions between fantasy and reality are clear, the connection is lost.

Spiraling galaxies contain the origins of life, hatched within the nebulae of gravitationally collapsing dust, gas and electrons. Stars form, concentrations of energy, emitting heat and light. Later planets, a cooling iron core surrounded by mantle currents, create an electromagnetic field, the spark of life.

Within the synaptic space of neurons or the interstellar space of nebulae, concentrations are a cloud, ions drifting in cerebral fluid or stars in galactic dust. Continuously collecting and thinning, moments of lucidity and cloudiness, the creative moment is a pairing, juxtaposition of an existing point of view with a foreign condition. Comparing them, differences are exaggerated boldly, while similarities focus on the nuance between. An original, independent idea is an illusion. Creative energy is relational. To channel it necessitates associations, connections, blending of two, energy and current. The tendency is to diffuse, so definition becomes meaningful. Distant or weak, a return to the sea blends life a new, overflowing at the source it collects in recesses, corners, cracks. Simply provide space, tuning to the pairing occurring naturally.

Though we are mostly water, we no longer feel the tides.

People go to great length to mask stars only visible at night. We fear what we don't understand or can't explain, myth and religion become a substitute for science. And our longings for the security and comfort of our childhood leave vacancies in our being. Architecture becomes the alteration we create to define reality as something we can live with, changing our environment to suit our needs, a bird nest made of temporals.

But our distortions of reality separate us, numbness to our surroundings and reality will not be ignored, concrete cracks, no matter how we configure it. Our best bet, to work with it, focusing on the subtle things, the occasional weed growing up through the crack. At a smaller scale, reality seems manageable and maybe we will find the strength to have indifference toward society, rather than ourselves.
So what if socks do not match? We simply need to stop, non-being, to see things as they really are, just outside our shaded windows and closed doors. Insight comes quite easily in the doing.

Architecture must be imbued with our being, our lost memories, releasing them when we inhabit, to reconnect, *circular singularity*. A pairing, balancing our being with our ancestral habits, our childhood creativity, our home.

Villa Vuoto is one of those pairings, the dream of a child,
              the manifesto of an architect.

288

A dedication
to my inspiration and continuous source,
my partner for a journey through life,
and mother of our two children,
Julianne.

Since the first day, you felt my nature, understood, accepted.
Where night and day would softly follow one another, your eyes
were a gentle force of nature, ordering and pacifying all of me.
To become not the object or end of my physical or intellectual
activity, but a pretext for my dreams, hopes, deeds.

Without the day we met, Villa Vuoto would not be.
More importantly, the person I have become would not exist.
In your face I recognize my own, the one of my childhood.
Before that day, you were my being
and in that moment I found you,
I was round again.

Not long after that day, Julianne's grandmother told of a place,
where sunlight radiates from below, deep in the recesses of a
grotto washed by the color of the sea.

A few moons later, a honey moon, we ventured to such a place,
back in her homeland, to relive her grandmother's memories,
now locked away in the blue mosaics of our home.

Independent mind and nuanced sensitivities,
the thought of Julianne gives me confidence.
Before all else, she inspires me. In awe of her complexities.
Under her spell, she challenges me, pushing me to the edge,
then reassuring, to keep me from loosing hope.
In the end, she provides insight, into a part of me I never would
have known without her patience and repeated efforts.

Thank you for being my true horizon.
Our home is defined by the space created between us.
My debt is eternal.

Contributors

Julianne (motivation & liberty to experiment)
Prescott Cole (land realtor)
Arthur Smith (closing attorney)
Bob Vester, National City Bank (construction loan)
Ann Novak, Meyer & Eckenrode (builders risk insurance)
Jill & Roy Cheran, neighbor (sub-division developer)
Tim Phillips, Franklin Park Borough (building inspector)
Schutte Surveyors (stake house footprint)
Emery Tree Service (clear house footprint)
Pete Debaldo, Debaldo Excavating (rough excavation)
Sherry Haule, Montgomery & Rust (excavation equipment)
John Martin, Jaymar Construction (footing excavation)
Hilliard Excavating (sewer excavation)
McCandless Sanitary (sewer line tap)
Penn Power (electric service line)
Equitable Gas (natural gas service line)
West View Water (water service line)
North Pittsburgh Telephone (telephone service line)
AT&T Broadband (cable television service line)
Bruce Edwards, H.P.Starr (construction lumber material)
Three Rivers Steel (footing reinforcing bars)
Bill Valesky, Valesky Homes (framing)
Donna Fenic, L&E Concrete Pumping (concrete pump truck)
Bob Yeske, 43rd Street Concrete (footing concrete)
Ed Thaner, E.A. Thaner (survey foundation pins)
R.I. Lampus (concrete block)
Ed Queen, Chief Contracting (foundation block work)
Thrower Concrete (foundation wall concrete)
T-n-D of Pittsburgh (foundation waterproofing)
Coco Aggregate (gravel backfill)
Mark Sample, Sample Development (built-up drive)
Pittsburgh Structural Clay (glazed fireplace brick)
Atlas Clay & Metal Products (firebrick, flue liner & mortar)
Alan Milliken, Milliken Brick & Stone (mortar color)
Forrest Steel (steel beams & columns)
RigidPly Rafters (exposed glulam beams)
Allegheny Crane (set steel & glulam beams)
Mill Direct (Anthony Power glulam posts & beams)

Matt Zottola, Zottola Steel (plates & angle brackets)
Dave Younge, Felx-Ability Concepts (Flex-C Angle track)
Bert Vosters, Vande Hey Raleigh (barrel roof tile)
Cassady Pierce (rubber membrane roofing)
Joe Young, Manor Roofing (barrel tile & flat roof work)
York Spiral Stair (circular staircase)
Ron D'Alesandro, Kellner Millwork (stair treads)
Anthony Phillips, A.Phillips Hauling (dumpster)
Tim Allwein (debris cleanup)
Bill Dudek, Bennett Supply (Tyvek Stucco Wrap)
Scott Rudolph, Iron City Sash & Door (windows)
Les Heffron, Andersen Windows (windows)
Chuck Stein, Allied Millwork of Pittsburgh (exterior doors)
John Walter, Iron Eden (door hinges & stair railing)
Habitat Hardware Emporium (exterior door hardware)
Rick Haarbauer, Exterior Products of Pgh. (Senergy stucco)
Harry Stites, Steel City Plastering (stucco & Venetian plaster)
John Crawford, Crawford Refrigeration (HVAC work)
George Gazzum, G&G Plumbing (plumbing work)
Walt Kotermanski, Oliverio Electric (electrical work)
Chris Meinert, Meinert Engineering (structured wiring)
Andy Imro, U.S. Spray Systems (Icynene spray foam insulation)
Wholesale Builders (blueboard)
Energy Reduction Specialists (Wirsbo radiant heat tubing)
Tim Nolan & Donny Weber (concrete slab work)
Barbara Sargent, Kemiko (concrete floor stain)
Louise Pascale, W.T. Leggett (kitchen cabinetry)
Thomas Schlueb (finish work)
Rocco Perla, Perla's Appliance Plus (cooktop, hood & sinks)
General Electric (kitchen & laundry appliances)
George Fischer, A&S Carpet (carpet floor)
John Russel, Russel Rolls (closet rods)
Michael Terral, Stickley (furnishings)
Magnificent Manufacturing & Sarah Miller (mosaic tile)
Shari Bennett, Bennett Design Group (vanity bowl)
Beth Fay Lane, Splash (plumbing fixtures & glass hardware)
Daneal Ferraro (glass accessories)
Target (glass curtain plates)
William Earl Kofmehl III (interior door hardware)
Tadao Arimoto, Arimoto Design & Woodworking (int. doors)

Chronology

CONSTRUCTION

438 trees cut & broke ground
439 stacked rocks (entry)
440 building permit issued & poured footings

443 completed block foundation
444 set first floor deck steel beams
445 set second floor deck glulams
446 set roof deck glulams

450 framed walls, laid fireplace & set front door
451 roughed-in mechanical ductwork
454 roughed-in plumbing and electrical wiring
455 fabricated steel stair railing

458 poured concrete floor slabs
459 completed interior plastering
460 stacked rocks (hillside) (om)
462 completed exterior plastering
463 moved in & hosted subcontractor thank you party

474 set entry gate

502 completed master bathroom (glass curtain)

545 set master bedroom door

Contents

AOAD

052 OM

Made in the USA
Middletown, DE
17 March 2023

26794713R00051